HEALING M.E. NATURALLY

9 Steps to Recover from
Chronic Fatigue and Fibromyalgia

Paulette Kumar

Best of health

Paulette Kumar

2019

Healing M.E. Naturally
www.paulettekumar.com
Copyright © 2018 PAULETTE KUMAR

ISBN-13: 978-1-98754-952-2
ISBN-10: 198754952X

Cover Illustration Copyright © 2018 by 10-10-10 Programme
Cover design by Waqas , waqas@bookcoverartist.com

Publishing paperback edition April 2018

Disclaimers

Limits of Liability and Disclaimer of Warranty
The author and publisher shall not be liable for your misuse of the enclosed material. This book is strictly for informational and educational purposes only.

Warning – Disclaimer
The author and/or publisher do not guarantee that anyone following these techniques, suggestions, tips, ideas or strategies will become successful. The author and/or publisher shall have neither liability nor responsibility to anyone with respect to any loss or damage caused, or alleged to be caused, directly or indirectly by the information contained in this book.

Medical Disclaimer
Always consult a doctor before undertaking any of the advice, physical treatments, exercise or supplements suggested in this work. While every attempt has been made to ensure medical information in this book is entirely safe and correct and up to date at the time of going to press, the author and publisher accepts no responsibility for consequences of the advice given therein. If in any doubt as to the nature of your condition or its severity, please consult a qualified medical practitioner. The medical or health information in this book is provided as an information resource only and is not to be used or relied on for any diagnostic or treatment purposes. This information is not intended to be patient education, does not create any patient-physician relationship, and should not be used as a substitute for professional diagnosis and treatment.

Legal Disclaimer
The information provided in this book is designed to provide helpful information on the subjects discussed. This book is not meant to be used, nor should it be used, to diagnose or treat any medical condition. For diagnosis or treatment of any medical problem, consult your own physician. The publisher and author are not responsible for any specific health or allergy needs that may require medical supervision and are not liable for any damages or negative consequences from any treatment, action, application or preparation, to any person reading or following the information in this book. References are provided for informational purposes only and do not constitute endorsement of any websites or other sources. Readers should be aware that the websites listed in this book may change.

Table of Contents

Dedication

To Corky, the most fabulous husband
who supported me throughout my journey.
To Kiertan and Saffron,
for your beautiful spirits, which kept me going.
To mum, dad, and my bro, family and friends,
thank you for your love and support.
Most of all, thank you God
for allowing this dream to come true.

Foreword

I first met Paulette Kumar when she attended my book writing course, and I was amazed at her enthusiasm for writing this book and helping you to recover from the devastating effects of Chronic Fatigue, M.E., and Fibromyalgia.

Healing M.E. Naturally explores 9 different ways that you can approach your own healing. Paulette is living proof that, when these changes are implemented, healing is possible. Paulette is now excited to share her holistic techniques and wisdom with you.

Healing M.E. Naturally provides many valuable insights into how you can begin recovering from debilitating chronic illness. In this book, Paulette explains exactly how you can recover from the illnesses that are taking away the joy from your life. By implementing the lifestyle changes she discusses, both she and her clients have dramatically recovered from the worst effects of their illnesses. No longer will you be housebound. No longer will you be bedridden. No longer will you live in despair.

With approximately 95% of the world's population suffering with illness, and over 400 million worldwide who suffer from the illnesses Paulette speaks of, I am certain that this book will help you of not only Chronic Fatigue, M.E., and Fibromyalgia, but of other chronic illnesses as well.

I am so excited about this book, and I know it will be the first of many brilliant books for Paulette, that will give incredible lifestyle changes and insight into how you can stay well by listening to your body, treating your body better and adapting yourself in order to heal faster.

Raymond Aaron
New York Times Bestselling Author

Acknowledgements

There are so many people that have supported me on this journey. These include my fabulous immediate family; darling husband, Kulvinder, beautiful children, Kiertan and Saffron, my mother, Magnora, father, Horace and Trev, who has been a great brother. I would not have been able to recover as quickly as I did without their constant emotional support, love, encouragement, hugs, financial support and so much more.

Althiea, my soul buddy from we were teenagers, who introduced me to my husband over 25 years ago and helped us both while I was ill with her acts of kindness. Coming at Christmas time and putting up the decorations each year with the children, and all the other visits you made, travelling hundreds of miles. Thank you.

Prabha, for being the best of friends in so many ways since our time at college, and over the past 30 plus years. Thanks for all your visits, the gifts and for loving me the way you do.

Anne, who would drive two hours just to take the kids out, when I couldn't, and all the holidays, fun experiences and other beautiful times we've shared together.

Denise, who has been my friend since I was 21 and still counting. For being a true sister. Taking me out of the house, especially at times when I was going through depression. For all your support when I turned to you for advice and for coming to meetings or anything else I invited you to.

Paulette G, who would spend hours on the bus to get to my home just to spend a few hours with me. Your beautiful words of wisdom will always resonate with me.

Charlie, a very special lady, who would remind me on a constant basis to believe in myself. She encouraged me to take the 'S' off my chest and called me more times than I can remember, when I was at my lowest.

Heather, who was a great encourager and supported me when I started my first business, even when I was ill. You were willing to get your hands dirty and help me in many different ways. I still can't believe you came and did some painting just before our guests arrived for that initial business meeting. You are one special lady.

Faith, I will never forget how you supported us when you came to York for Kiertan's singing in York Minster Cathedral, and for that very long night when Saffron's friends slept over for her birthday. Thank you too for all your acts of kindness throughout my journey.

Melanie, part of the sisterhood of friends, who came and gave gifts, especially to my children year after year. Thanks for all you've done to support me over the years, especially while I've been in Sutton Coldfield.

Donna H, for taking Saffron on days and nights away. Thank you to you, and your mum, for all of your support over the years.

Khembe, for coming to my house for the past 10 years to help me maintain my beautiful hair. For encouraging me and giving me advice and supporting my business ventures.

Acknowledgements

Sharon, for your yummy food, helping me to declutter and so many other things. Your generous spirit has been such an encouragement.

Norma, thanks for our Monday chats and your support and business advice.

Sereena, thank you for being in my life when I needed a friend. You have a special place in my heart and I will always love you.

To all my spiritual mothers: Mrs Elwin, Mother Hall, and Sister Myrie (as we call her). These mothers who pray for me and treat me as their own. This also includes Velma, my spiritual mentor, who has been a huge encouragement over recent years.

Michelle, Christine, Savita, Jane thank you for your support, your advice and inspiring me. From all our adventures together and fabulous meals out that ensure I was always well feed and watered. Thank you. To Margaret, Helen, Josh, Shaun, Dave and all the additional friends I've made from being a part of Salus, including Andy who would make my favourite gluten-free chocolate cake for my birthday each year. Thank you all. Our walks in the park helped me overcome depression and provided me with many special friendships.

Linda Jones, and the knowledgeable Ron, and all the staff, trainers and friends of Salus, including Hazel and Theresa, I am grateful for you coming in my life when I needed you most. I'm not certain if I would have recovered the way I did if Linda had not started up Salus for sufferers of Chronic Fatigue. An immense heart of gratitude is sent out to you always. My success is yours.

To my extended family who were there for me when I was low, including Auntie Julie, Uncle Gideon, Auntie Cherry, Sharon and Annie.

To all my Business Sisters and those who supported my business ventures, especially during my sick years, including: Shaheen, Linzy and Mark, Sandra, Doreen, Patricia, Tracy, Lucy, Carol, Sharon, Sue and so many others. All who helped me to believe in me again. Allowing me to do what I love best, enhancing people's lives.

To my neighbourhood prayer group: Liz and Rob, Pauline and Martin, Diana and Ian, Trevor and Sue and all the others who prayed for us and supported us.

For all the people in Bethel, New Jerusalem and Sutton Coldfield Baptist Church (SCBC); Donald, Neil, Paul and Beth, who help with the children. Denise, Rachel, Sue, Liz, the Karens', WaiYee, Rev. Eve Pitt prayer group and my Bible Study Fellowship (BSF) friends: Suzy, Sue, Hayley, Sarah, Rebecca, Joanne, Kim, Linda, Liz, Lynn and Lynne and all my other church support.

I never knew such kindness existed until I was at my lowest; the food cooked, flowers given, food delivered, moral and financial support given when we needed it. Thank you church family. Especially for the anonymous money in the huge envelope that came through our door in a time of need. You proved that all the sowing my husband and I did in other people's lives when we were able to, meant a lot, and that we were worthy of reciprocation.

To Narinder, Deep, Debra, Nirmla, Den and Dhaminder for coming to be with me, when I could not travel to our reunions. I wonder if we had anything to do with Jimmy Spices being closed down because of our massive discounts?! Lol! Narinder, thanks for the massive helping hand.

Acknowledgements

To my life coach and mentor Lynne Lee, thank you for trusting and believing in me. You taught me online while I was in my bed the tools I needed to become qualified in Life Coaching, so I could fulfil my dream of doing the job that everyone told me that I naturally did. I will always be grateful to you for helping me to take the massive leap of faith towards a career that makes my heart sing. You made a complete stranger into a special friend.

Those that helped me to keep my home in order including: Maj, Marva, Sonia and Vikki.

For all of the therapists who treated my body and worked with me to get myself well: Sister Peters, Sansia, Warwick, Pete, Ruth, Ron and Sharon and all the others. You not only treated my body, but my mind and spirit. I will always be grateful to you.

To all my team, especially Shushana. You have been a tower of strength and an amazing ally, who I can depend upon to get me through. Without you my business would not exist the way it does. I have the best people in my team. Thank you for the tremendous support from Debra, Becky, Lashay, Precious, Katherine and Emily, without whom my book would not have been so well written.

To all the parents that supported me with my children, I will never forget your kindness. Often picking up Kiertan and Saffron, bringing them home from school, clubs and other activities when I was too ill myself. To Helen who has remained loyal for so many years and my adopted God-daughter Izzie. To Don and Di, Cathy and Nana, Lisa and Craig, Louise, Julie, Linda, Racheal and all your husbands. Robyn, Karen, Gill, Sonia, Katie, Rachel, Nikki, Yvonne and everyone else, a special thanks and appreciation to you.

Thank you Rose and Arthur, who encouraged me when I was going through my depression. Rose, for giving me your keyboard so I could teach myself something new, which really did take my mind off things.

Thank you to all of the staff at Moor Hall, who were gentle with me and became my friends during my period of illness. A special shout out to Dave, Pedro, Lorenzo, Connie, Mel and Paul.

Access to work: Raj, Dale and your colleagues. Thank you for acknowledging my disability and providing me with support. This project has definitely been successful because of you.

I thank Mr. Raymond Aaron, New York Times Top 10 Bestselling Author, my book coaches, Naval, Dyann, Liz and his team for assisting me with my book.

I know that there are others that have supported me however, I cannot put everyone here, otherwise the list would be far too long. I love you all. To anyone I've forgotten, please forgive me for not specifically acknowledging you. You know who you are, and God knows too.

Chapter 1

The Overcomers

"Recovery is something that you have to work on every single day, it's something that doesn't get a day off."
Demi Lovato, American Singer

Illness Has No Respect

Illness has no respect for anyone. It can intrude in your life suddenly, without any warning. It affects the young and old, the rich and poor. No one is ever prepared to be ill. Sickness, however, comes to most, if not to all. Have you ever experienced a headache, stomach problems, debilitating pain, irritable bowels, problems with sleep, fatigue, difficulty concentrating, memory loss, joint stiffness, anxiety, depression, mood swings, panic attacks, breathing irregularity, dizziness, a fever, dehydration, a sore throat, a foggy head, problems with your speech, eye problems, sensitivity to light, sensitivity to noise, sensitivity to odours, loss of balance, problems with weight, tenderness all over your body or good, old fashioned flu symptoms?

Many people have suffered from at least one of these conditions at some point. Amazingly, these are all some of the symptoms that a person suffering from Chronic Fatigue Syndrome (CFS), Myalgic Encephalomyelitis (ME) and Fibromyalgia experiences. I should know, as many of the hundreds of people I connect with have experienced these symptoms, as well as myself. I suffered from most of these symptoms for almost a decade. This book tells you how several of my clients and I have overcome the tyranny of these symptoms, through natural remedies. We have recovered from being bedridden, housebound and barely able to walk, and are now experiencing life to the full again; a new life without the use of pharmaceutical drugs. By taking a holistic approach to improve your mind, body and spirit, you can be an OVERCOMER too.

According to research found in Science Daily, over 95% of the world's population has health problems. About half of all adults have one chronic health condition. According to the Centre for Disease Control and Prevention, one in four adults has had two or more chronic health conditions. There are over 400 million people, worldwide, who suffer with ME and Fibro. That is a lot of sick people.

This book, *Healing M.E. Naturally*, is for you if you suffer from these chronic illnesses, or if you know someone who wants to improve their physical, mental and spiritual well-being.

Are you one of these people? Or, do you know someone who is unwell, and you want to make a difference to their lives? If the answer is yes, then you will love this book.

What are Chronic Fatigue Syndrome and Myalgic Encephalomyelitis?

Chronic Fatigue Syndrome (CFS) is a medical condition, but the cause of it is not yet known. Very often it comes with a fever, prolonged aching, extreme tiredness and depression; typically occurring after a viral infection. Myalgic Encephalomyelitis (ME) has similar symptoms to CFS; however, it is characterised by damage to the brain. Myalgic Encephalomyelitis causes damage to almost all vital bodily systems. It is, primarily, a neurological disease, so it interrupts the way your brain works, and it also affects your blood vessels and circulation.

For the duration of this book and for the ease of you, the reader, both Myalgic Encephalomyelitis (ME) and CFS conditions shall be referred to as ME, although I appreciate that the conditions are not identical.

People from all different types of backgrounds and walks of life experience ME. It does not discriminate based on gender or age. This illness affects children, adolescents and adults of all ages. It is most common in people between the ages of 40 and 60 years old. Statistically, women are affected more than men. White people are diagnosed more than other races and ethnicities. However, many people with ME have not been diagnosed, especially among minorities. Some of the reasons that people have not been diagnosed are because of limited knowledge of the condition and the symptoms associated with it, limited access to healthcare and a lack of education about ME among healthcare providers.

People with ME are often not able to do their usual activities. At times, ME confines sufferers to bed. An early sign of the condition is having overwhelming fatigue that is not improved by rest. ME may get worse after any activity, whether it is physical or mental. This symptom is known as post-exertional malaise (PEM). Many people with ME do not look ill but will have many of the symptoms mentioned above or have problems with sleep, thinking and concentrating, pain, and dizziness.

What is Fibromyalgia?

ME is often experienced alongside Fibromyalgia, also called Fibromyalgia Syndrome (FMS). Throughout this book I will call it Fibro. Simply put, it is having pain all over the body. Fibro is a rheumatic condition characterised by pain and stiffness in the muscles, joints and tissues. This sums up what I experienced for many years. It felt like having arthritis-type symptoms all over my body. The pain that comes from Fibro can be intense. It is this intense pain that highlights the difference between suffering, solely, with ME and also suffering with Fibro.

Effects of ME and Fibromyalgia

People who suffer from ME and Fibro can experience a whole variety of symptoms. For some it is like experiencing the worst flu symptoms; pain all over your body, a groggy head, but no runny nose. I guess that is why, in the past, ME was referred to as 'yuppie flu,' because it mimics the signs of the flu and was often experienced by young executives.

For many of my coaching clients, the illness starts with a virus. The body's immune system becomes low, and before you know it, without any warning, it brings you down. Your body seizes up and you are hardly able to move. Some people say that it came upon them shortly after an operation; others cannot explain where the exhaustion and immense pain originated. There is not enough evidence to really know how it all begins.

What is so strange about this illness is that no two people will necessarily have the same signs or symptoms. Many of us become sensitive to light. I was like Count Dracula's wife, having to stay in the dark all the time. I felt my way around a pitch-black room, rather than turning on a light or opening up the curtains. For others, sensitivity to noise can be their main symptom. That is why it is so difficult for people in the medical profession to help those of us who suffer. We have so many symptoms that differ and mimic other illnesses.

The Worldwide Statistics relating to Myalgic Encephalomyelitis, Chronic Fatigue Syndrome and Fibromyalgia

	ME	CFS	Fibro
Illness statistics	It is estimated that ME is experienced by more than 250,000 people in the UK, and approximately 1 million people in the US. Other countries are now also producing figures.	There are over 34 million people worldwide that suffer with CFS.	According to the National Fibromyalgia Association, 3-6% of the world's population have Fibro. With a world population of over 7 billion, this estimate would mean that somewhere around 400 million people worldwide have Fibro. In the UK, the NHS estimates that 2-5% of people in the UK may have Fibro, based on a UK population of approximately 65,500,000. This would mean that approximately 3 million people in the UK have Fibro.

Famous Sufferers of These Illnesses

I am here to tell you that you are not alone. There are many of us who experience chronic illnesses, and even some of the most famous people in the world suffer from ME, CFS and Fibro.

Florence Nightingale, the famous British army nurse and Red Cross pioneer, displayed the symptoms of CFS and Fibro and was said to have suffered for decades. Morgan Freeman, the A-list Hollywood actor, and Michael Crawford, the entertainer, have both experienced the extreme pain of Fibro. Legendary film director, Blake Edwards, who directed such classic films as Breakfast at Tiffany's and The Pink Panther, was diagnosed with ME and stated of it: "The desperation for me was enormous." The Irish singer Sinead O'Connor had to take a three-year sabbatical from her music career to battle the symptoms of Fibro. The 'Believe' singer, and all-round song diva, Cher, has suffered from CFS. Even the bold and brash Lady Gaga had to cancel some of her tour dates because she was in hospital, suffering from an intense attack of Fibro. It is believed that Job, from the Bible, suffered from Fibro too. It is quite astounding to see how much these chronic illnesses have impacted people throughout history.

Discover What is Inside This Book

Throughout *Healing M.E. Naturally*, you will discover aids, tools and techniques to apply to your life, which will help you to recover. You will learn how to address depression, which is so prevalent in anyone suffering from a chronic illness, and find out about natural remedies and techniques that will help you to manage your time, pace yourself and eat yourself well again. We will address solutions to sleep problems and the spiritual aspects of your life, which are vital to your recovery process. Throughout this book, will be many of my health tips to calm your mind, bring health to your body and feelings of upliftment to your spirit. In chapter 2, you will discover how I became ill and my own story of recovery from ME, Fibro and depression.

Notes

Chapter 2

My Journey

"Recovery begins from the darkest moment."
John Major, English Prime Minister

How I Became Ill

It started with flu-like symptoms. I was weak and very tired. The doctor told me it would last for two weeks. Several weeks after that, I went back to the doctors, experiencing extreme tiredness, aches and pains all over my body and my mind could barely function. The feelings just would not go away.

My Dark Days

Do you have children? I have two beautiful children whom I love dearly. Suffering from a chronic illness, when you are a mother to two young children, is extremely tough. My children were just toddlers at the time. "You cannot hold mummy's hand, but you can hold my little finger," I said to my daughter as she reached for the safety of my hand before we crossed over the busy road. That day it was far too excruciating for my three-year-old to hold me by my entire hand. I had struggled to even get out of the house to take her shopping for a few essentials. She was there, holding my finger, showing me love, and I was wishing I had stayed at home. Her constant dialogue wearied me. I loved listening to her, but not that day. That day I could hardly think, brain fog was happening again. To walk and talk was like climbing a mountain. This was my Mount Everest. How incredible it was that after weeks of resting I still had such little energy, not enough even to go out for just an hour.

Health tip for the mind: Now, I communicate more honestly about how I am feeling, and you should do the same.

It took 15 minutes to get to the shops, 30 minutes to shop and another 15 minutes to get back home. The rest of the week, I would remain lying down, recovering. Such was the challenge of my fatigued and pain-ridden body. Seeing the joy on my daughter's face was my reward, and all that she needed was an hour out with her mum, doing something special. The price I paid to see that smile was immense. Can you imagine being so ill that no one can even hold your hand? Have you ever been so tired that by exerting yourself, ever so slightly, meant days and weeks of bed rest?

Doctor's Visit

The following week I had a trip to the Barberry, a hospital unit in the Queen Elizabeth Hospital in Birmingham. A trip that was too daunting for me to take by myself. My husband escorted me, as I would sometimes stumble as I walked. Today he was my chauffeur, my eyes and my walking aid.

"You are too weak to watch television," the consultant said. "Too weak to just sit and watch tv?" I questioned. "That is ridiculous!" Yet in the back of my mind I knew it was true. For even sitting at home watching television would leave me depleted. "If light and noise are bothering you, then you need to sit in the dark, with as little stimulation as possible. Watching television will take some of your energy away and you cannot afford to lose that right now." So here I was being given permission to sit and do nothing all day long. All day long... and these felt like the longest of days.

No Need to Go Out to Work

Even though it felt, at times, that I was going out of my mind having to be still, I must admit, it was good to be off work. Work had been particularly demanding, and it felt like a blessing to be able to take a break from the stress. I remember the presidential elections taking place in the USA, and it specifically caught my attention as it was potentially the first 'Afro American' ever to be elected. I stayed awake that night for as long as I could, to see the results. 'This is great,' I thought, not having to go into the office the next day. It meant I could sleep in. The US election results were not disappointing, but I paid the price of staying up for those results. The price was paid the next day and the next, and the day after that, with even more pain and fatigue.

The Challenge with Pharmaceutical Drugs

How could I eliminate this pain? The pain was intense, in fact, it was excruciating. I had barely any energy whatsoever. How could I get my energy back? I then had difficulty sleeping too. I mustered enough energy to go back to see the doctor, who prescribed more medication. I went from one pill, to the next. I was prescribed Amitriptyline, which is usually used for depression, but in small doses it is also used for pain. I had Gabapentin and Temazepam to help with sleep. Most of the time the medication helped and gave some relief, but it also numbed the functioning of my mind.

Feeling Suicidal

I was told time and time again, to rest. I had been doing nothing but this for months. The months were now turning into years. I started to think more and more, 'Life should not exist in this way.' Things began to get progressively worse. So much time had passed since being diagnosed with a 'virus' and I still could not shift the feeling of fatigue and pain that I was experiencing all the time. I was losing hope. I knew I was not supposed to think that way. I had been brought up in the church and no good Christian person should ever think, 'there is no point in me being here.'

Health tip for the mind: Tell someone about how you're feeling. Do not suffer in silence.

It was the lowest I had sunk to, and it scared me that I felt like that. I caught how I was thinking and I stopped it. The prospect of my children living without a mother came flooding to my mind. What was I thinking, how could I leave these precious souls? My family kept me going despite it all, but boy was it was a struggle.

Focusing on Being Positive

Every morning I awoke and felt like I had not slept at all, and once I had crawled to the toilet to relieve myself, I would crawl back into bed. I listened to whatever positive affirmations, or inspirational messages that came my way, anything to take my mind off the pain. 'I am healed, I am well, I am whole' is the affirmation that I used time and time again when I was too ill to walk and too depressed to think about everyday living. I was desperate and did not know what to do with myself. I believed I could be healed, but my body did not feel that way.

To keep my mind staying positive, I tried healing visualisations. I was guided to imagine myself feeling better, seeing myself doing the work I longed to do; motivate and empower people all over the world through motivational talks and my bestselling books. While visualising myself feeling better and happier, I made every effort to make those positive feelings sink inside my heart and my bones, until the pain and depression I had been struggling with became fainter, even if it was for just a moment or two. As I practiced this, over time, I became more and more energised and felt more confident that I would be able to conquer the world, even if from my sick bed!

I now teach my clients how to write and practice saying affirmations that are specific to them. I also teach them how to visualise themselves well again. To learn how to write an affirmation and to use the visualisation I did go to my website: paulettekumar.com and search for 'affirmations' and 'visualisations.'

My journey of recovery from ME and Fibro began when I discovered fantastic remedies where medical science had failed. This was the moment of enlightenment! There are some key elements that can help you on your journey to recovery, specifically tackling depression, that we shall explore in the next chapter.

Notes

Chapter 3

Step 1 – Depression

"Depression begins with disappointment. When disappointment festers in our soul, it leads to discouragement."
Joyce Meyer, Spiritual Leader

Address Depression First

There is one symptom that seems to be common among many of us with ME and Fibro and that is depression. British artist, Giles Andreae, stated of depression: "Here is the tragedy: when you are a victim of depression, not only do you feel utterly helpless and abandoned by the world, you also know that very few people can understand, or even begin to believe, that life can be this painful. There is nothing I can think of that is quite as isolating as this."

When I was at my worst I was advised to address my depression before I could address the physical aspects of my illness. This was rather surprising, because I did not realise that I was depressed. Depression can happen to anyone. It is even more intense when you are fatigued and in pain. You are unable to concentrate, have a lack of energy and low mood, you are disinterested in doing anything and, on top of all this, you suffer with feelings of guilt. These symptoms often tend to be recurrent, with many of my clients, and have a significant effect on their everyday lives.

Herbal Alternatives

My client, Margaret, had counselling to address her depressive symptoms, followed by a series of Cognitive Behavioural Therapy (CBT) sessions, which are more solution-focused and clinically structured. These sessions began to address some of the deep-seated issues that had perhaps caused her to be ill. She had to learn how to face her problems head on, some that had bothered her for many years. When she found the courage to address past challenges, she realised that she had a lot of tension, which was causing acidity in her body. Too much acid build-up causes rather extreme fatigue. She had to learn to calm her mind, a real problem for many people with these chronic illnesses.

Health tip for your mind: use aromatherapy oils to boost your mood and relax your mind and body.

Margaret was advised to take pharmaceutical medication, but she found these to be mind-numbing and did not like the reaction they had on her body. She described the feelings as "losing touch with what was going on around her." Not the state of mind needed when you have young children. She decided that there must be alternative methods that would aid her recovery. That is when she searched, and she found me; a Life Coach that specialises in helping people to recover from ME and Fibro.

I began to help Margaret to look at herbal alternatives for depression, ones that I had discovered for myself. St John's Wort can be used as an anti-depressant and there are herbal teas like camomile and valerian that can be used to calm the nerves. Herbal tablets which have l-theanine, valerian, passionflower and lemon balm in them are said to reduce anxiety. These became a regular part of Margaret's diet, and helped to improve her sleep.

One of my coaching clients uses Ashwagandha, which is an herb from ayurvedic healing, that has been demonstrated to be as effective as some tranquillizers and anti-depressant drugs. Specifically, oral administration of Ashwagandha, for five days, is said to have anxiety relieving effects similar to those achieved by the anti-anxiety drug, Lorazepam, and anti-depressant effects similar to those of the prescription anti-depressant drug, Imipramine. It is always good to check with people who are skilled to understand these alternatives more; a nutritionist, naturopath or other types of health professional may be able to help.

You can also use mood-enhancing oils like lemongrass and bergamot on your pillows. Adding a drop to a diffuser in your home, in your bath or anywhere else will help lift your spirits and relax your mind.

Get Some Warmth and Sunshine

Sam, another client of mine, would rarely leave the house. When you are depressed you often stay indoors for weeks and months, or, in extreme cases, years. Lack of sunlight is often linked with depression. When Sam was too weak to go out and walk, I suggested she sit in the garden with a light duvet in the colder months. Getting fresh air and sunshine are vital in recovery from depression.

Health tip for your mind: Keep crimson flowers in your sight. Seeing something scarlet can actually give you a burst of energy. So, get some red flowers in your home!

A lot of people with ME and Fibro are deficient in Vitamin D. Vitamin D can be obtained from being in the sunshine and is essential for a healthy mood. If you live in an environment that experiences less sunshine, then it may be wise to begin taking a Vitamin D supplement.

Visit my website: paulettekumar.com to find out more about the benefits of supplements.

Heating up the body is a great way to help reduce muscle tension, anxiety and relax the mind. It is said that sensations of warmth may alter neural circuits that control mood, including those that affect the neurotransmitter, Serotonin. Serotonin can affect mood and social behaviour, appetite and digestion, sleep, memory and sexual desire.

You can get warmth to the body in lots of different ways. If you do not have a nice warm beach to lie on, an alternative is to have a warm bath, filled with Magnesium salts (Magnesium Chloride). Otherwise, you can use a sauna or a steam room. Jacuzzis are great; however, you must be wary when using them. Jacuzzis, like a bath, will let you absorb what goes into them. So, a communal jacuzzi should be approached with caution.

The Happy Chemical

Depression is made worse by dehydration, so make sure you drink plenty of water. But it is also linked to a lack of Serotonin. Serotonin is a chemical that nerve cells produce. It is found mostly in the digestive system. Serotonin mainly affects your mood, appetite and sleep.

The advice I give to those who attend my conferences and seminars about obtaining Serotonin, if their levels are low, is to include these in their diet: 5 HTP, Vitamins B6 and B12, St. John's Wort, lots of fresh air and getting sunlight and Vitamin D.

Exercise and Support

A lack of activity and tiredness helps to maintain negative thinking, which feeds depression and then makes you not want to do anything. And so, the cycle goes. I would advise you to do some movement every day, even if it is only a little. Despite feeling depressed and tired, if you maintain making small amounts of movement, it will help you feel better in the long run.

Health tip for your mind and body: Do a little dance to your favourite song every now and again. Remind yourself what it is like to have a little fun!

One of the most significant parts of my recovery from depression was doing gentle exercise. When I first started, it was really difficult to motivate myself because of the fatigue and all of the pain that I was experiencing. Eventually, I started to go for walks with a group of other sufferers. Having a reason to get out the house, being in the fresh air in the park, among the trees, and sharing with my fellow sufferers; Michelle, Christine, Savita, Jane, Margaret, Helen, Andy, Dave, Josh and Shaun, made me feel alive.

When you discover that so many people around you are going through the same trials, you start to feel less depressed because you know that you are not on your own. A burden shared is a burden halved. Meeting and talking with others WILL make you feel less depressed. I would really recommend that you find others who are able to support you. Even if this is online, you can support each other from a distance (you can join my online community on Facebook). This may be your only option at first. Find what works for you and be courageous enough to get support for yourself.

Cognitive Behavioural Therapy

Cognitive Behavioural Therapy (CBT) helps you identify the unhelpful ways you can think or act, that lead you towards anxiety and anxious episodes. CBT, by identifying these triggers in your brain, attempts to realign your thinking, which makes positive changes and therefore reduces your pain and fatigue. It breaks the brain's sometimes vicious cycle and stops you from being consumed by your thoughts before pain or fatigue makes you crash.

I was introduced to a course of CBT by my doctor. It helped me to identify how my thoughts were limiting me, which then caused stress in my body. The stress resulted in pain and more fatigue.

CBT teaches you how to change and even challenge your thinking. It helps you to move away from a potentially depressive episode, and instead aids you in harnessing your thinking and seeing things from the real perspective. You learn how to see situations and thought processes in a different way. This helps create self-belief and builds you up so that you no longer allow negative thought processes to gain ground in your mind. I would recommend a course of CBT to anyone who is going through some depression.

Health tip for your mind: Dress up in bright colours (especially warm ones) and wear what makes you feel good, as it will help to boost your spirits.

It can be a long journey back from depression, but it is possible. When you begin doing some of the things you enjoy again, it will feel wonderful and freeing. However, make sure you are still taking things slowly and pacing yourself. I will show you how to do this in the next chapter.

Notes

Notes

Chapter 4

Step 2 – Pacing Yourself

"Adopt the pace of nature: her secret is patience."
Ralph Waldo Emerson, American Poet

Learning About Pacing

Working at your own pace is vital to recovery. One of the biggest lessons I was taught on my journey to being well again was learning how to manage my own time and pace myself.

Pacing teaches you to focus only on the tasks that are really necessary, and the need to eliminate others. Often you have to use the art of delegation in every area of your life. I have had to learn the hard way to take that 'S' off my chest, as my friend Charlie has constantly reminded me: "You don't have to be the heroine any more. You don't have to act like Superwoman."

Health tip for your mind: Take off your time piece. Do not wear a watch and just listen to what your body says.

The Art of Delegation

I would strongly advise you to do only the tasks that you need to. Especially when you are not well. Find people who can do specific tasks more effectively than you. Delegate what needs to be done and give yourself peace of mind. If you manage a home or even staff at work, you must get away from the feeling of 'having to do it all yourself.' Get to know your strengths, weaknesses, energy drainers and limitations, and trust others to do some of your work. That is the way to get better. Stay focused on the most important tasks and get your children, partner, friends and work colleagues to help you with the others.

Pauline's Pacing Story

My client, Pauline, did not pace herself well. When she spoke to me, she would regularly say that she was at work, exhausted, and was looking forward to taking a break. Turns out the 'break' she was looking forward to was when she had to take time off for a pending operation. The operation would get her out of work and give her a few weeks to be able to rest.

A possible reason for Pauline becoming chronically ill may have been due to having a minor operation, from which she found difficult to recover. She knew that her body did not feel right before she went into surgery. Not only was she exhausted, she was suffering from a cold, possibly even the flu, but she honestly thought that an operation was the only plausible reason she could take a few weeks off from work. When the nurse came to see her, with the paperwork for the operation, which asked questions about her physical state, Pauline ticked the box which stated that she was 'well.' Big mistake. She then had to go back to work, utterly drained and exhausted. It took her months, instead of weeks, to recover. This was the beginning of a downward spiral of ill health for Pauline.

Recommended Pain Management

A year later, Pauline was back in hospital. This time it was because she was in a lot of pain and her doctor could not find its source. She was given drugs to try and help with the pain. After days and days, and a variety of tests, the pain subsided, but did not go away. That is when the consultant said: "We do not think that there is anything else we can do for you. None of the scans we have done show what the cause of the pain is. With the use of pain killers, the pain is better so we are going to send you home and refer you to a pain management clinic. You may just have to live with this pain." Pauline was not pleased. She had come into the hospital with pain and was leaving with pain. Though, the referral to the pain management clinic did lead her to one of the greatest lessons she learnt during her recovery, how to pace herself.

It took Pauline a while to realise that she had been overdoing things for years. Her profession lent itself to having lots to manage, like so many other people in management. Pauline had the biggest to-do list ever. Any one day, she could have 20-30 things she wanted to achieve, placing far more tasks in her daily schedule than she could physically manage. But what was she to do? Everything needed doing... Or so she thought.

When Pauline was still trying to fit everything into her schedule that she wanted to do, her body began to feel really tired. When she asked for advice from her nearest and dearest, she was told: "Just push through it. After all, everyone has lots going on..." She began to feel resentful and hated it when anyone asked her to do anything for them. Did they not see that she had enough on her plate? Her commute to nursery, to school, to work, to the kitchen and to bed, was more than enough. Her biggest dilemma was that she did not know how to stop and say "No." That was when she found me, a Life Coach who could help her.

I was able to help Pauline because I had suffered similar experiences and setbacks. My becoming ill forced me to assess my priorities. I reached a point where I acknowledged that I had to take the time to stop. I started to assess what I was doing and why I was doing all of my weekly activities. My body could no longer cope with doing everything anymore, so I had to be particular about what I incorporated into my days and weeks.

Assessing Priorities

Prior to being ill, I had never heard the term 'pacing' before. I had heard of time management in my capacity as Project Manager, where I learnt how to manage my work time. However, outside of work there was always so much to do: managing personal matters, family, extended family, the house, incorporating friends and the unexpected, such as the car accident my husband had, all took up space. I had to learn how to personally pace myself, with family, work, church and everything else and say "no" to a lot of things, even if this was difficult for me.

Health tip for your mind: Try not to be controlled by other people's time. It is okay to delay a decision or not to do something until you feel up to it.

Managing Pain

Pauline learnt about pacing through the pain management clinic. The physiotherapist told her that there were some people who will always need to live with pain. She, like lots of others with Fibro, would perhaps be one of those. If you have pain that cannot be cured, you have to learn how to manage your pain, and the biggest part of pain management is learning how to pace yourself. Pauline was placed on an eight-week course which taught a dozen people how to live with pain, pace themselves, help their families understand the pain and begin exercising.

This new phenomenon of pacing showed Pauline and I that we had to look at everything as a whole, then decide what was important and what was not. That was really difficult for us, because everything appeared to be important at first. My journey and Pauline's were very similar and we both struggled, initially, with adopting pacing into our lives.

Putting Pacing into Practice

How would you decide if you had to choose between showering or having breakfast when you are experiencing pain or extreme fatigue? You may even have to choose which most basic of tasks to do. Pauline understood full well that if she did not learn how to pace herself, she would be constantly tired and in pain, and this was not the way she wanted to live. So, she started to assess all that she was doing and tried to identify the things that she could take out of her life, with the hope that perhaps one day she could go back to the things she wanted to do.

For me, when I was at my worst, I knew I could not take out my immediate family; they were a constant that had to remain. So, what could I exclude? I had to identify what took away a lot of my energy. I gave up television, listening to music, reading and I turned my phone off, as it was all too loud and stimulating. Cooking, washing up and laundry were too physical. I didn't go shopping; my husband, church and friends did. I still showered but it took a lot out of me. Essentially, if I managed to even get down the stairs, I would lie on the sofa, in the dark, in silence, all day. That was how bad it was.

Health tip for your body: Get more excited about your shower by using a natural shower gel that both makes you feel good and has a smell that excites your senses.

You Are the Priority

When I began to get advice from the pain management consultants, instead of giving me more advice about things to exclude, they asked me to include something else. Something important. Time for me. Time for me to attend to myself and combat the tiredness and pain that I was experiencing. This was the only way that I could live a reasonably happy life. I needed to look after myself. I thought I was, but I realised it was not enough, and so I began the journey of looking after myself 'well' not just 'enough to get by.' I let the feelings of guilt go. This is what I now teach my clients and all the people that come to hear me speak at conferences and seminars.

It is important to schedule in time for rest during the day. Once you start implementing pacing into your life, you may find it difficult at first (actually, expect it!), but it is important to persevere. You WILL start to see the difference it makes. Making pacing a priority in your recovery will be a big step to you feeling happier and healthier. In the next chapter, I will talk about stress and proactive ways that you take captive stressful thoughts and sensations, so that they will not negatively affect your life.

Notes

Notes

Chapter 5

Step 3 – Eliminating Stress

"With all that's going on in our lives and the world,
reducing stress is important."
Andie MacDowell, American Actress

Starting to Eliminate Stress

Many people who are ill feel a lot of stress. Stress is our emotional and physical reaction to pressure. This can be exacerbated by new life events and family or work pressures. Be they self-inflicted or inflicted on us by other factors, remember it is not unusual for seemingly happy events to make us feel stressed. For example, Christmas, moving house, getting married, parenthood, etc. It is all about how we manage these stresses. During times of stress, it is common for your thoughts to be negative.

Common stress-fuelled thoughts:

- I cannot cope
- This is too much
- This is unfair, someone should be helping me
- I do not have enough time
- I must get this done

Emotions:

- Irritability
- Anxiety
- Impatience
- Anger
- Depression
- Hopelessness

Physical Sensations

The body automatically sees stress as a threat, so produces adrenaline as a response. So, our heart starts racing, we breathe faster, the muscles in our neck and shoulders tense up, we get hot and sweaty, experience headaches and difficulty concentrating, get forgetful, agitated and restless, we can even have bladder and bowel issues.

Health tip for your body and mind: Take a 10-20-minute nap during the day, as this will boost your energy levels for the rest of the day and help your brain to take a break.

Behaviour

When we are stressed we rush about, we are unable to settle, we have lots to do but feel unable to finish them or see how to, we shout, we argue and we are unable to sleep. We eat more, some of us use drugs or smoke or drink more and we can have occasional emotional outbursts.

Methods of Combatting Stress

Vitamin C is the great anti-stress vitamin. When you are stressed you have sweet cravings, so we naturally assume we need sweets, sugary additions, cakes, pastries and chocolates, when this is not, in fact, the case. It is your body telling you that it needs Vitamin C. Most, if not all, things in nature that contain large amounts of Vitamin C are sweet.

The Magnesium in your body is depleted in times of stress. Magnesium helps to maintain a strong nervous system, and is essential for energy production, enzyme activation, strong bones, relaxed muscles and sleep. In terms of Magnesium supplements, I use a cream, oil, spray and some salts for the bath, which I have found wonderful. These added supplies of Magnesium have helped to calm my body and keep my muscles relaxed. I order them from this website: morgangenus.com.

Other alternative therapies may help provide some additional benefits in times of stress too. Simple things like a massage, having your hair done or a facial etc. Taking a short break away from everyday life can help. You are also getting your 'you' time.

It is so important to stay in control and eliminate as much stress as possible. Some stressful events cannot be controlled, but a good well-being life coach can help you to manage a lot of them.

When in a stressful situation, stop and think of how to manage it. Those first few minutes will help so much. Consider: What changes can I make? What exactly is making me stressed? Often, when you look from outside the situation you see things much more clearly. This gives you time to consider your reaction.

There are always a few points to check first. These will help you understand your true thoughts:

- What am I reacting to?
- What is the worst that can happen?
- Is it worth it?
- Am I over thinking things?
- Am I deliberating over something that is not as bad as it seems?
- Is there real pressure or am I putting pressure on myself?

Always try to stop, view and breathe, then make a plan or set goals on how to handle the situation. Do not rush in. Ultimately, you could save yourself from the worst effects of stress, panic attacks, overwhelming anxiety and suicidal tendencies, if you learn how to manage stress at the first signs of its approach. This will not come overnight, but if you get support and put these things into place early on you will be far happier and a lot less stressed in the long term.

Health tip for your spirit: Practice forgiveness, of yourself and of others. When you forgive, you are letting go of the things that can bring you the most stress.

Taking as much stress out of your life as is physically possible will help to reduce the fatigue and pain you feel. When we are under stress we do not usually eat well. Nutrition, however, plays a large part in our recovery. We begin to look at this in the next chapter.

Notes

Notes

Chapter 6

Step 4 – Eating Yourself Well

"I naturally favour a clean, healthy diet.
A salad sandwich is one of my favourite meals!"
Victoria Pendleton, Olympic Cycling Gold-Medallist

Nutrition

You are what you eat. I have discovered that your wellness is often dependent upon what is going on inside of you. You can be more energised and feel less pain if you eat more nutritious foods.

Food has been a major part of my recovery from ME and Fibro. In fact, it has become one of my favourite parts of my recovery: the focus on looking after myself and my diet. You know how some ladies like to go out to shop for clothes, shoes and makeup, and some men like to shop for the latest gadget or a nice car? Well, I get excited about shopping for the best foods that will keep me well. I would advise you to embrace the nutrition side of your recovery too.

Health tip for your body: Eat more protein than carbs, because it makes you feel fuller for longer.

The Importance of Nutrition

In the beginning, I really did not know that food was so important, and the sad thing is, I was convinced that, prior to being ill, my diet was good. However, when I became ill I learnt that it needed to change, big time. I had to readjust my food intake, my supplements and the things I drank. It became a whole new science and way of living for me.

Finding Energy from Food

When you are fatigued, ill or in pain you need to take extra special care to let food fuel your injured body. We all know that we get energy from food, but I began to realise that I was not getting enough energy from the food I was having, so I started to explore this. I began to keep a journal of what I was eating and the effects my food would have on me. For example, I noticed that if I had wheat products, not only did I begin to feel sluggish, but a dull pain would start to develop at the roof of my mouth.

At this point in my recovery, I was too ill to go on the computer to research. I noticed that technology would drain me of energy. When I began to have the courage, strength, motivation and energy to get up and go out, I attended lots of seminars about diet, food and supplements. I wanted to find out how they could help to energise my body and relieve me from the symptoms of ME and the pain that comes with Fibro.

I learnt that the way energy from food is converted into energy for our bodies is through the power engine of our cells, called the mitochondria. Mitochondria are the cell's power producers. They convert energy into forms that are usable by the cell. So, if the mitochondria are working well, then we can get more energy. At first it was all too much for me to take in. It took me a while to understand, especially with my foggy head. Mitochondria was a new word and a very big word at that! The one thing I did understand was that if you feed your body with what is needed, it would be guaranteed to give you energy.

If you are not giving your body the right levels of energy that you need, you will not be able to function well, and you will become debilitated and sick. According to research, the average daily intake of food does not give you enough of the most vital nutrients you need. You need a much larger intake of Omega 3, Iodine, Zinc, Calcium, Magnesium and B Vitamins, and when you do not get these into your body you set the stage for chronic disease.

Health tip for your body: Omega 3 fatty acids found in food like salmon improves your mood, brain function and helps some people to avoid a midday slump. There are plenty of supplements too. Vegetarians can have flaxseeds.

Foods I Cut Out of my Diet

I cut out processed food. The fresher my food is the better I feel. As I have already said, I cut out wheat as it made me feel sluggish, my mouth and throat area would hurt and my brain did not function as quickly. So, I tried eating some of the gluten-free foods that started to appear in my local supermarket. Some worked, and some did not. I found some, like the lovely lemon and poppy seed gluten-free slices, caused me to be even more fatigued. When it comes to gluten-free food it is going to be a case of trial and error for you. Try a few different foods, from a few different stores, and see which foods and stores work for you. Monitoring how you feel after you have had the food is the best way to discern its success. For me, Marks & Spencer stocked my favourite gluten-free food: bloomer bread, cake, fruit pie, crisps and some frozen products.

I decided to cut out dairy, as I heard it was not so good. I cut out milk and ice cream, and reduced my intake of cheese. Instead, I had almond milk and dairy-free ice cream, whenever I wanted a treat. I began to explore which cheese had no milk. I found goat's cheese at first, but realised that this has dairy in it, so I turned to sheep's cheese and found that by using these alternatives the inflammation in my chest started to be reduced. It was hard for me to cut out eggs, as they had been a part of my staple diet for many years. So, I experimented, cutting out eggs for a couple of weeks, to see if it would make any difference. What I found is that when I reintroduced them into my diet, I began to feel like I would vomit. I tried free range eggs and the reaction was just the same.

My friend Andy, who also suffers from ME and Fibro, was told to take out egg yolks from his diet. I tried this and found, occasionally, I could have egg whites without feeling ill. I found that my throat would not hurt so much when I cut down on the dairy, but any time I introduced the dairy back into my diet I developed pain in my throat area again.

In terms of drinks, there are definitely some drinks to include in your diet and some that you should avoid, as they will impede your recovery.

Health tip for your body: Eliminate regular tea and coffee from your diet, as they drain your energy. Replace them with water or herbal alternatives.

I discuss both the beneficial and unbeneficial drinks for ME and Fibro sufferers on my website: paulettekumar.com.

I no longer use microwave ovens because I found out that they are not good for your health. Heating up your food in the microwave can actually zap the food of its nutrients. Vitamin B-12 is destroyed in food heated up in the microwave. Vitamin B-12 keeps the nerve and blood cells healthy and helps to prevent a type of anaemia that makes people tired and weak. Microwaves also create carcinogens in food (when you heat food up in plastic containers), which can be damaging to your health. Eating food from a microwave oven can also change your heart rate and the makeup of your blood (increasing your white blood cell count but decreasing your red blood cell count, which is not good!). I now advise all of my coaching clients to refrain from using microwaves.

Brilliant Foods

Sulphur-rich foods support your brain, your body's cells and your liver and kidneys. Sulphur is also good at detoxifying the body. It can be found in the cabbage family: broccoli, cauliflower and spouts. Onions and mushrooms are also rich in Sulphur, although I was told not to eat certain types of mushrooms as these are fungi and the stomach may not be able to digest them well. Other coloured vegetables are also good, particularly carrots and peppers.

My client, Yvonne, found that avocado would neutralise a lot of the acid build up she had in her stomach. Brightly coloured fruits are very good for you. I was told by my naturopath to cut out bananas, as these have a lot of sugar and are fattening. I did not have the energy to work off any extra pounds! Raspberries and blueberries have been my go-to fruit and I have them with my mid-morning gluten-free porridge, alongside apples, pears and nectarines.

Have in your diet a dinner plate of green leaves rich in B Vitamins, and Vitamins A, C, K and minerals. There are a lot to choose from: spinach, broccoli, parsley, other greens; however, kale has more nutrition per calorie than any other green plant. B Vitamins will protect the mitochondria and your brain cells. Vitamins A and C support the immune cells. Vitamin K keeps your blood vessels and bones healthy.

Fibre

The gut is said to be the centre of good health. If you eat foods from all the colour groups, every day, you will be consuming many healthy nutrients that will help your body to recover. Yellow/orange fruits and veggies (butternut squash, carrots, lemons, yellow peppers etc.) contain lots of Vitamins A and C and antioxidants. The green group (cucumbers, limes, broccoli, asparagus, zucchini) have plenty of fibre and high sulphur levels in them. The purples/blues (aubergine, grapes, blueberries, plums, purple cabbage) are some of the most nutritious foods. They help protect against cancer, memory loss and urinary tract infections. Red fruits and vegetables (tomatoes, red peppers, red grapes, radishes, red onions, pomegranates) are full of antioxidants and lycopene (fights cancer). The nutrients in the white group (cauliflower, onions, garlic) lower blood sugar, feed probiotics and have brilliant anti-inflammatory and anti-bacterial properties.

Health tip for your body: Snack on carrot, celery or cucumber sticks, broccoli and cauliflower instead of eating crisps, cakes or biscuits for a quick bite to eat.

Fat

We all need fat in our diet. It may have bad press, but we do need some. It is the quantity and type that should be considered. The good fats, which have Omega 3 and 6 essential fatty acids, are monounsaturated and polyunsaturated. Omega 3 and 6 are essential in your diet. Omega 6 is found in vegetable oils, seeds and nuts, and Omega 3 in leafy vegetables. A ratio of 2:1 for these nutrients is considered good. Bad fats, from fatty meats and full-fat dairy produce, are not inherently bad; it is just a case of eating them in moderation. However, trans fats, found often in highly-processed cakes, pastries and fast foods, are bad for you, so I would recommend taking these out of your diet as much as possible. They will make you slow and lethargic and may cause you more pain. Especially in your throat.

Other Healthy Foods

In order for me to restore my energy levels, I began to eat organ meat, which is rich in Iron. I, mainly, ate lamb's liver for a while. Studies have shown that organ meat is good at supporting your cell function, which produces more energy. Various animal hearts and tongues are other organs people eat in order to gain more energy. I have not tried these. These types of meat are good for vitamins, minerals and Co-enzyme Q10. Omega 3 fatty acids can be found in fish; wild fish such as salmon and herring and grass-fed meat, like lamb.

Seaweed is good for iodine and the brain needs this for removing toxins and keeping cholesterol lower. It is also great for reducing the risk of breast cancer and prostate cancer. For those of us with ME and Fibro, having it just once a week would be extremely beneficial.

Health tip for your body: Add beetroot to your diet, it helps lower blood pressure, fights inflammation, boosts stamina and supports detoxification.

When I began to realise that my body was extremely acidic, and I had to neutralise my body, I took meat out of my diet. I started using a natural remedy of virgin apple cider vinegar. For more information about the benefits of apple cider vinegar, go to: paulettekumar.com.

Financially, it can be a huge jump in food costs when you eat healthy and stock up on organic vegetables, fruits, fish, and organ meat, but the result of changing your diet means that you can have a much better quality of life. You can live again. In my own life, I have started my own business and I am writing my books and talking to people from all over the world, because I have the energy from my food supply to do so.

It is all trial and error. Work out what is right for your body and makes you feel good.

Supplements

Supplements play a major role in maintaining a good immune system, possibly enough to stop a virus if the right nutrients are present or ingested early enough. The trick is to keep good nutrition maintained long-term, to have a build-up of immunity to fight off possible infections. The danger is that when we are stressed we do not look after ourselves properly, and this reduces the immunity, leaving gaps in our immunity for attacks from toxins and viruses. So, even when you are having a more stressful day, keep taking your supplements so that your immune system remains strong.

You need to protect your cells too, and this can be done with fish oil and Co-enzyme Q10. What your cells need, to start producing energy, are B Vitamins, Sulphur and antioxidants. As well as taking additional supplements, find out what foods you enjoy that contain these and start increasing the amount of those foods in your diet too.

Good supplements and your food intake can help you to recover from chronic illness more quickly. Looking at nutrition, and applying changes to my diet, definitely brought about a dramatic change in my healing.

Another piece in the jigsaw puzzle of recovery is finding out how to get better sleep, another major problem for those of us who suffer from ME and Fibro. We will find out more about vital techniques that will improve your sleep in the 'sleep' chapter coming up.

Notes

Chapter 7

Step 5 – Sleep

"We are not healthy unless our sleep is healthy."
William Dement, M.D. Ph. D Stanford professor
and pioneer in sleep research

The Problem with a Lack of Sleep

We all know that sleep is important, but it is even more crucial for those of us who suffer from ME and Fibro. Not having enough sleep can have a great impact on your immune system, coordination and mood. When you are sleep-deprived you can experience what seems to be a 'brain fog.' What many sufferers call a 'foggy head.' This is when your brain does not function on all cylinders. Lack of sleep can make you irritable, anxious and difficult to live with.

The cumulative lack of sleep will add up to sleep debt. When you are sleep-deprived you are at a higher risk of depression, hypertension, diabetes and obesity, among other illnesses. The way to get rid of the debt is to pay off the debt. Every time you ignore the body's demand for payment, you lose payment through your energy stores. It is important to increase the amount of sleep and rest you have, so that you can place more sleep and rest in the body's bank.

How to Sleep Well

Getting enough sleep to regain your energy levels is a whole science in itself. It is important to prepare your body, mind and spirit for good sleep. It is also important to sleep at the right time. Taking control of when you eat and what you eat is vital for good sleep, and sleep hygiene is also crucial. I will talk more about this later. Often people with our illnesses find it difficult to fall asleep or stay asleep. I experienced both. I have learnt how to get to sleep quickly and stay asleep, without the use of medication such as Temazepam or herbal remedies. It took some time to figure out how to do it, but I did.

Health tip for your body: Start by trying to go to bed one hour earlier than you normally do. Then ensure this becomes your new routine.

One of the greatest discoveries, for me, to help me recover from sleep deprivation, was getting to sleep at the right time. I advise people on my coaching programme to get to bed by 10pm, as this is the time that we get the best sleep. I usually try to get to bed for 9pm. I then reflect on the day by writing what I am grateful for in my gratitude journal, pray and read something inspirational. All of this sets me up for better sleep. When I was at my worst, I found it difficult to do all of this. I did not know that there was a right time to sleep or a best time. This is called REM sleep and I will discuss this further in my next book, *Healing Naturally*.

Sleep Hygiene

Preparing your environment for sleep is called sleep hygiene. There are a number of factors in our environment that can help us or deter us from sleeping well. Noise can be a problem when you are ill with ME and Fibro. Lots of people who suffer from these illnesses have a great sensitivity to noise. So, having certain types of music or noise around you can be distracting and prevent you from having good, quality sleep.

Health tip for your body: Don't be conscious of yawning! Yawning is the body's way of cooling down the brain and this decreases the stress and pressure we feel.

Taking away as many noises and distractions as possible will help you. My client, Shaun, found that having calming music playing helped to soothe him to sleep. You can also have a calming, soothing recording of a soft voice that encourages you to relax and helps you to fall to sleep quicker. This is material that I have made available to some of my coaching clients and they have found that falling to sleep is much easier. If you would like to learn more about making a peaceful recording, or where to purchase a good one, then you can find that information on my website: paulettekumar.com.

Your room should feel relaxing and conducive to sleep. That means getting rid of those electrical distractions, devils, sorry, devices out of your room! Getting rid of those devices can make a big difference to your quality of sleep. I took them out of my room once I learnt that they could impact on my health. I took out all the mobile devices, I did not leave the television or anything else on standby and I switched them off at the mains. Thinking I was well enough, I did introduce the devices back into my room. I found that once I had slept with them there, I started to feel unwell again. So now I know that it is better for my health to keep my bedroom technology-free.

Prepare Your Mind for Sleep

As well as preparing the room where you sleep, it is important also to prepare your mind. Watching a documentary about death, or people acting out violence, is unlikely to lend itself to a relaxing night's rest.

Watch your thoughts also. My mind used to conjure up lots of thoughts and I found it difficult to stop thinking. Even when I did not realise I was thinking, I was. So, I had to find ways of calming my mind. I discovered that journaling or some focused thinking or meditation did the trick. Taking your mind away from your everyday thoughts, worries and concerns and staying focused on positive things really helps calm your mind. My coaching clients often tell me how much they love to hear my meditations, which I have created especially for them. These meditations will vary from talking through a guide to relax their body, to being taken to a place of deep relaxation that mirrors their personal favourite place.

Listening to calming music or meditations is brilliant, because you can download them onto an electronic device such as a phone or tablet. This means that they are portable, and you can listen to them anywhere. Once you start to fall off to sleep, it is best to place the device on flight mode or switch it off. Or if you are fortunate, like me, to have someone that goes to bed later than you do, then ask them to make certain they switch it off and place it outside the room. If your partner goes to bed earlier than you, then it is a good idea to still have your meditation playing through your headphones. Eventually, you will be able to get to sleep without the need for calm music or a meditation, like I do now.

Eat Well and Sleep Better

Your diet is one of the keys that opens the door to better sleep. The time we eat and the things we eat can really have an adverse effect on our sleep. It is said that it is better for you not to have food too near to your bedtime. Perhaps, leave a gap of two hours, prior to going to bed, so that your body will not feel full and bloated. Your stomach will also not have to digest food that you have consumed just before going off to sleep, which uses up your energy.

That sounded ridiculous to my client, Richard, at first, because if he did not have food soon before going to bed, he would feel hungry during the night. It was when he discovered that his big problem was that he was not having enough food during the day that he started to change his eating schedule, and his cravings for food at bedtime disappeared. He changed his schedule, so that he was having five small meals a day. Even if two or three of those meals were one big meal divided up. He just spaced the food out and had extra fruit or vegetables: carrot sticks, cucumber, pears or some other raw food snack in between meals.

I changed my eating schedule too. One of my own saving graces was being able to make a juice in the morning that was big enough to be drunk over the whole course of the day. Thank God for the NutriBullet! It saved me time and energy, and the roughage made a huge difference to my energy levels each day. I still have one almost daily. I even took my Nutribullet aboard with me recently, when I was going to be away from home for a few weeks. A few of my favourite NutriBullet recipes are available on my website.

Health tip for your body: Have warm water before anything else, in the morning, to flush away the toxins.

When I do not have the energy to make a super-duper veg or fruit smoothie, I use food replacement substitute drinks, such as Herbalife. In the early days, when I had no energy to prepare juice or make a meal, the shakes really did save me for many months. I will always be thankful to my friend Heather who ordered them, got them delivered to my home and even showed me different recipes.

So, eating and keeping full during the day will often prevent you from waking up at night, because your body does not need the fuel. **No cookies and milk, please!** I have found that the cleaner you eat (raw, fresh food), the better sleep you will have. Kiwi fruit, cherry juice and lettuce all have a sleep-inducing effect on the body. Some of you may or may not choose to eat prior to bed, but if these foods help then maybe it is worth a try. The cherries, in particular, help stimulate the production of Melatonin, the hormone that helps get you to sleep.

Sleep and Physical Exercise

Doing a small amount of exercise and going out doors really does help you to sleep better. You have to be very careful about the amount of exercise that you do, when you suffer with these illnesses. Exercise, nonetheless, is very important. Ten minutes outdoors can make a world of difference. One of the exercises that I would recommend is a stretch technique that is used in Qigong. Yoga and Qigong are slow physical exercise practices, with deep breathing, that you can practice when you are not well. Practicing Qigong (pronounced Chi-gong), taught me to treat my body gently and to use slow and deliberate movements to start to bring life back into my body. Qigong is similar to Tai Chi and is great when you have been inactive for a long time. *I want to emphasise that I do not take on the spiritual aspects of these practices. I simply use the physical exercises that bring me the physical relief that I require.* When you go to my website: paulettekumar.com you can find videos where I give you a demonstration of my stretches.

You will find that a little, strenuous exercise helps you to sleep better and keeps your body fit and agile and free from seizing up. So, it is really important.

Health tip for your body: Exercise a little, at a time, according to how you feel, rather than do graded exercise. Often graded exercise is too much and causes setbacks.

Sleep and Breathing

Doing breathing exercises can increase the amount of sleep that you have too. Breathing correctly is a great way to help you overcome the effects of stress, both on the body and within many other aspects of health. Within the usual areas of focus, which mainly consist of what we eat, drink and how much we exercise, we rarely consider how important breathing correctly actually is. I bought a salt pipe (from online) in order to breathe deeper. On my website: paulettekumar.com there is a blog post which gives more information on the benefits of using a salt pipe and some breathing exercises you can try. After using my salt pipe and learning how to deep breathe for over a year, I developed a much more relaxing sleeping pattern.

Medication and Sleep

If all of the above techniques do not work for you, then you may want to consider taking medication. This is something you should discuss with your doctor.

At first, I used the medication from my doctors before I knew everything I have told you about. I used various drugs including Amitriptyline and Temazepam. The medication would often make me feel like a zombie. When I woke up and tried to function, it was difficult to think. I found one that was not so debilitating that I used for pain relief and that was Naproxen. The only problem with that was it can cause heartburn, indigestion, nausea, and I developed a facial rash. Overall, I felt the need to try herbal alternatives, rather than to depend upon these pharmaceuticals, with their side effects.

Herbal Alternatives

Valerian is a perennial flowering garden plant from Europe and Asia. It has scented white or pink flowers and the roots of certain varieties are used as a dietary supplement, commonly thought to have sedative effects and help with mild anxiety. I tried a variety of herbal supplements from my local health shop. After a year or so I found an herbal tablet called Melissa Dreams, with lemon balm, which helped me sleep better.

Practical Steps

Sleep is essential for body maintenance and repair. It is said that the golden time for sleep is between 11pm and 3am, as this is when your liver function is best restored. It is also believed that sleep before midnight is worth two hours of your sleep after that time. If you are affected by light and noise, maybe consider what seems obvious: blackout curtains, sleep masks, ear plugs, and ensuring a new or comfortable mattress and pillows are available etc. The list is endless, but it is so beneficial to know that there are so many aids to a good sleep.

In the next chapter, I will spend some time sharing with you the spiritual aspects of my recovery and I will also give you some ideas of how you too can benefit from these.

Notes

Chapter 8

Step 6 – Spiritual Awakening

"When wealth is lost, nothing is lost;
when health is lost, something is lost."
Billy Graham, American Clergyman

Approaching Spirituality

When you are unwell, and seeking recovery, I believe that you should leave no stone unturned, you should rule nothing out without trying it. My spirituality has been a significant part of my journey and recovery process.

Why Many People Turn to Prayer for Healing

The definition of a prayer is a solemn request for help or an expression of thanks, addressed to 'The Divine.' Many people question what prayer is, because they don't know how to pray. Prayer, however, is one of the most natural and instinctive human responses.

In a recent survey, asked what it would be for, if they were to pray, 31 per cent of respondents cited peace in the world, followed by an end to poverty (27 per cent), a family member (26 per cent) and healing (22 per cent). While 5 per cent said they did not know what they would pray for, 14 per cent said they would never pray.

To many people, prayer seems complicated, but it really does not have to be. Prayer is a simple means of communication between us and 'The Divine' (God), that allows us to interact.

I am often asked: "How do you pray?" or "What should I say if I pray?" However, this is something very personal and it depends on what you have going on in your life. If praying is new for you, in time, you will know what you want to say, and you will get a feeling of what you need answered. I find praying a joy, as I am talking to my best friend! It is easy to talk to someone when you know they love you. It is an opportunity to be truthful, express your worries and concerns and to be thankful for the little milestones you accomplish along the way.

How to Pray

- Take a few moments to stop what you are doing.
- Pause and relax.
- Picture the scene that you want to communicate about. For example: think about yourself being well and healthy.
- Make your request for healing to God, in your heart (inside) or externally (speaking, writing, singing...).
- Believe and trust that healing will take place. This may not be immediate, as it was not for me, but keep having the faith that it will occur. I did, and this hope kept me going in my darkest of days. It served me well, because I believed and 'I'm now healed, well and whole' again.

Regular prayer was a big part of my upbringing. God is my best friend, who I go to in times of great need and joy. "True prayer is neither a mere mental exercise nor a vocal performance. It is far deeper than that – it is a spiritual transaction with the Creator of Heaven and Earth." Charles Spurgeon, British Clergyman.

All relationships need to be nurtured, and a relationship with God is no different. It helps if you are in regular contact with Him. Talk about your thoughts, as you would to those closest to you. Prayer does not have to be loud; it can be silent. But by opening the lines of communication you are opening your mind and heart to many good things, feelings and emotions.

Health tip for your spirit: Pay attention to your spiritual growth, as this will give you optimism, joy and enthusiasm for life.

So, what are the benefits of praying, reading the good book, 'The Bible' and spending time with God? The benefits are really quite extraordinary. When we pray, not only do we unburden ourselves and let go of a lot of our stress, but we reveal our problems to God, the one person who knows us better than we know ourselves. And we can come to Him with an *expectation* that He will make our lives easier if we ask Him to.

In the Bible there is a reading where God says: "I alone know the plans I have for you. Plans to prosper you and not to harm you. Plans to bring you hope and a future." As a believer, I trust that my future is bright and that He will free me from my struggles.

I appreciate that not all of you will know God, rely on God or even believe that He exists, but for me not to take the time to tell you how God has helped and strengthened me would be to hide from you a great and available source of healing. Spirituality is not only about getting to know God more, it is about getting to know yourself more too, and finding ways to encourage, strengthen and liberate yourself from life's hardships.

Alongside prayer, the most significant spiritual help I received during my recovery was practicing mindfulness.

Mindfulness

Health tip for your spirit: Practice mindfulness and ditch multitasking.

Mindfulness concentration and focus thinking helped me to learn how to stop over-analysing things, and, instead, to enjoy the moment. It was introduced to me by Linda Jones, who helped many people in my area who were suffering from Chronic Fatigue. I did several courses, but I admit it took me a long time to get it into my head. *Again I want to emphasise that I do not take on the spiritual aspects of Mindfulness, but I do use the practice techniques.*

Mindfulness meditation is a practice that is particularly effective in calming the mind and taking away anxiety. An important part of mindfulness is reconnecting with our bodies and the sensations they experience, even if those sensations are pain and fatigue. This means waking up to the sights, sounds, smells and tastes of the present moment, whatever they may be. That might be things as simple as looking up at the stars in the sky, listening to the sound of birds chirping outside, inhaling the sweet aroma of the cake baking in the oven and feeling the polished surface of the banister as you walk downstairs.

Another important part of mindfulness is an awareness of our thoughts and feelings as they happen moment to moment. It is about allowing ourselves to see the present moment as it really is and not denying feelings of pain and fatigue. It is about learning to accept exactly how you feel in that moment. When we do that, it can positively change the way we see ourselves and our lives.

Mindfulness really has made such a huge difference to my life. Being able to stay focused on the job at hand has been a wonderful gift. Thank you, Lord, for Dr Singh, at Good Hope hospital, who, in his spare time, had classes for people who suffered a lot with pain and other illnesses. He would teach us mindfulness techniques to help us to get well again. In that room, there were people with cancer, back problems, victims of trauma and lots of other sick people, with different types of illnesses. Through the techniques we were taught, we learnt how to live, with our varying illnesses, in a better and more positive way.

If you want to know, specifically, how I practice mindfulness and teach others who attend my seminars and conferences, then please go to my website. Another practice that will help you in your recovery is meditating.

Benefits of Relaxation and Meditation

Relaxation is the state of being free from tension and anxiety. It is important that you introduce relaxation techniques into your life for you to calm your mind and de-stress your body. Doing meditation is one way of relaxing. Meditation can help with stress reduction, insomnia, headaches, pains, overcoming addictions, improving self-confidence, improving relationships, lifting your spirit and keeping you looking young (lol!). Once you know the techniques, you can meditate anywhere and relax your body, without needing guidance. Meditation only takes 15-20 minutes of daily discipline and practice to reap the benefits.

You can relax by being still, listening to something relaxing such as music or a calming meditation.

Health tip for the mind: Meditate by listening to your favourite piece of calming music. The familiarity and comfort you get from the music will make meditation even more pleasing.

The focus should always be on what gives your mind a rest. I always take time out, around lunchtime, to relax my mind. I recommend to my clients that they implement time for relaxation every day into their schedule.

If you want to follow the same meditation regime that I do, then I have videos on YouTube that help with meditation and relaxation - search Coach Paulette Kumar.

Affirmations

Affirmations are one of those things that I rarely did, prior to getting ill. However, I found that they made a huge difference to my recovery. I went on a retreat and was taught how to write an affirmation. I was then encouraged to say it daily. In fact, several times a day. I tried it and, for the most part, it worked. It was not until I found an affirmation that totally suited me and my situation that I let it sink into my spirit and said it often. The best affirmation I said while I was ill was: "I am healed, I am well, I am whole." I am not certain why this one stood out more than any other for me. However, whenever I felt a little low I would say this affirmation over and over again. Affirmations are really good when you are feeling down or depressed. They give you hope.

Health tip for your spirit: Say a positive affirmation in the mirror daily.

I now teach my coaching clients to say an affirmation every day. They can say one that we create together or make one up for themselves, if they are happy to do so. So, in writing an affirmation, be specific to your situation. For example, my client Sandra wrote the affirmation: "I'm blessed and I have an abundance coming to me." Try writing one that translates to your life and your goals and dreams. Then repeat your affirmation several times a day, when you are feeling low but also when you are feeling good. You will be amazed when you start seeing the difference this positive self-talk makes.

Gratitude Journaling

I have been journaling for just over 20 years. At first it was just an outlet to offload my struggles. However, now I have a gratitude journal. This is where I take the time to stop and give thanks for what I am blessed to have, anything beautiful that I see and everything I enjoy and experience. When you begin writing things down, you start to realise how much there is to be thankful for and how beautiful the world can be.

Admittedly, journaling felt like more of a task than a delight when I was feeling really unwell. When you are exhausted or in pain everything becomes a chore rather than a pleasure. I still persevered with it, the best I knew how, in my dark days, and I am glad I did. This form of expression helped me to share in my journals what I could not say to anyone else. Even when some situations I experience seem bleak, by journaling and giving thanks, I am really uplifted.

Health tip for your spirit: In your journal, also make promises to yourself about things you want to do/achieve before you die. This will give you a focus, purpose and have things to look forward to doing.

I do most of my journal writing in the morning, as often in the evening I am too tired to concentrate. Do what is right for you. The primary purpose of my journals is to maintain conversations with 'The Divine.' I express to Him how I feel or how I would like to see things changed.

To accompany the spiritual aspects of your recovery, it is also important to explore the benefits of some physical treatments, such as lymphatic massages and acupuncture to help you reduce your symptoms. Read the next chapter to find out more about several treatments that will make a significant difference to your recovery.

Notes

Notes

Chapter 9

Step 7 – Physical Treatments

"The resistance that you fight physically and the resistance you fight in life can only build a strong character."
Arnold Schwarzenegger, Austrian Actor and
Ex American Politician

Benefits of Physical Treatments

Holistic treatments work to relax the body and mind, enabling the body's own natural healing ability to commence. Generally, the benefits of holistic treatments are relief from pain, fatigue and stress, and making you feel uplifted. On my recovery journey, I used various treatments, I had not used previously. Although I am pretty much recovered now, I still do a lot of these treatments on a regular basis.

Naturopath

I started off going to Ron, a naturopath, because he understood fatigue from his own journey. It was also amazing just being able to speak to someone about my fatigue and pain. Finding a therapeutic outlet can help you when you are feeling low. I found it comforting that he would really listen to me during the space of that 40-minute consultation time.

He recommended supplements, assessed what I was eating and told me to cut out lots of sugary things. I think this was because I was experiencing candida, a yeast infection found in my mouth. Candida can be caused by stress, a high intake of antibiotics and having sugar-loaded health drinks (in my case). These were quick, nutritional, food replacement drinks I would have as an alternative to cooking a full meal, but long term had a bad effect.

Lymphatic Massage

Lymphatic massage continues to be a key element of my recovery. Combined with body brushing it stimulates the blood flow in my body. Lymphatic massages help to improve the immune system and helps to fight infections by increasing the production of antibodies. I usually come out from my treatment, feeling full of vigour.

I recommended this type of massage to several of my clients, including Sharon, as it is gentle, and its prime purpose is not to stimulate the muscles but to drain any toxins from the body. Sharon found that every time she had one of these massages she was able to have deeper sleep. This was the best physical treatment Sharon had had since she was ill. After she discovered she would sleep so much better at night, after having a massage, she began to have them at home. Sharon would invite the masseur to come around in the evening, then, after the massage, go straight to bed. She continues to have lymphatic massages today.

Health tip for your mind: Reverse engineer your energy. When you are feeling less energetic, try to look energised. Act it out until you begin to feel it.

Osteopathy

I used an Osteopath for many years, who helped to stretch my body, especially as my body had experienced little movement over the years when I was bedridden. Osteopathy I found removes underlying pain. Pain and the stiffness in muscles and joints are reduced. Once I had a treatment, I found that I had an increase in the range of motions in my joints and especially in my back, which caused me a tremendous amount of pain.

The Osteopath also used a technique called cranio-sacral motion. A strange treatment but I went with the flow. It is a gentle non-invasive form of body work that addresses the bones of the head, spinal column and sacrum. This type of therapy helps to aid respiration, by releasing compression in those areas mentioned, which alleviates stress and pain. The combination of treatments helped me enormously.

Acupuncture

My client, Karen, had acupuncture, as many of the people she knew that were getting better had done. She found a great acupuncturist in Sutton Coldfield called Ruth, who not only treated her but would talk to her and help relieve the psychological pain that she was going through. Karen started having acupuncture once every two weeks (when she was really struggling) and now she only has it once every six weeks. She also tried Bowen therapy and colonic irrigation, to try and take all the toxins out of her body, and to see if that would help her to feel better. All these treatments added up to quite a bill, but Karen believes she would still be unwell if she had not had them.

Effects of Physical Treatments

You may experience any of the following reactions within the first 48 hours of having physical treatments: light-headedness, tiredness, headaches, increased energy levels, an increase in urination, nausea, emotional releases, aching joints, appetite variations and congestion of the nose or chest. So, for the first 24 hours keep things simple, as my client, Rachel, did. Follow her example and just drink more water, avoid alcohol, eat well but lightly and no excess physical exertion. Then, after the first day or so has passed, you should feel better. It will take your body time for your body to adjust.

In the following chapter, we will look at relationships and how, sometimes, our relationships can become strained as we combat chronic illnesses. However, I will give you some advice on how to nurture yourself, so you can have better relationships.

Notes

Notes

Chapter 10

Step 8 – Yourself and Your Relationships

"A person's pride can be their downfall, and they need to learn when to turn to someone else for support and guidance."
Bear Grylls, British Explorer

Relationships and Illness

I love my family and my friends, just like you do, but on this journey of recovery I had to learn to ignore the demands of others. I was always there for people who needed help. In my community and in the church, there is always someone who will want your time, money or whatever you have to offer. I had been brought up to practice JOY (Jesus Others You). What I have learnt, since being ill, is to nurture myself first, before I nurture others.
To be selfless is not the same as being selfish. BIG lesson for me on my journey of recovery. It took me a long time to believe it. How could I take care of myself and leave others behind? Relationships can be very one-sided. It is important that you ask to receive, as well as to give.

Family Relationships

Family were my greatest trainers, because they demanded, and I gave. I was trying to live up to the expectations of what I *should* do. I have learnt that, often, they did not need my help, or would even turn around and say, "I never asked you to do that for me!" What is it, about our upbringing, that makes us believe that we must be on tap? And keep giving and giving and giving?

Health tip for your mind: Help and acknowledge others when you can but learn to love yourself too and give yourself the gift of life.

Working Relationships

I also discovered that workplaces and their bosses are not designed to cater to our needs, they are there to cater to their needs and the needs of the organisation. 'No great insight' you may say, but I was really duped into thinking that the people I worked for cared for me and had my best interests at heart, always!

Perhaps there are some places, or there are some environments, where employers value deeply their employees and their health. However, with today's demands for more productivity in the workplace, I think there is less and less nurturing, caring and loving of employees, and more an attitude of 'let us get as much out of you as we can.' Employers want value for money; 'if you cannot do the work someone else will.' Often that demand is conveyed to employees, and if you do not bear through, then you will simply be replaced. This kind of pressure and stress is not good when you are not well.

Successful Relationships

So, the key to success in your relationships at home with your family, or outside in your workplace, is to do what is good and right for yourself first, and to give to others out of the extra that you have. Do not let people deplete you of all your resources and energy.

Health tip for your spirit: Ditch the energy vampires. Stay away from people who leave you feeling depleted.

Having a meaningful relationship must start with you loving yourself. If you do not, at least, try to love yourself, why expect someone else to? If suffering the effects of ME or Fibro leaves you feeling low in mood this can be very difficult, but you must try.

How to Put Yourself First

Firstly, it is important to know who you are, in order to understand your values and relationships. Ask yourself:

- What do I feel comfortable with?
- Why do I connect with some people and not others?
- Why do I pull away?

Setting realistic relationship goals will help you to focus on what is right for you, to take your life forward. To master the art of relationships we must be comfortable with the idea that we connect and disconnect with people all the time. Some of these connections will be long-lasting, others less so, but they all add something to who we are.

How you relate with people at home, work and with friends is very important. If you portray hate, anger and a dislike for life, it is very likely you will receive that back. But if you give love, peace and goodness, then these will come back to you.

Health tip for your spirit: The more good you give the more good you will receive. That is an old saying, but it still has a lot of truth.

In your own relationships, identify how you would treat others that are unwell. For example, you might say: I would be kind to them even if they are having a bad day. I would look after them, because I see their need. I would encourage their development. I would ensure they eat the right foods. I would make sure they exercise, to gain strength. I would tell them they are handsome/beautiful. I would raise their self-esteem and tell them how important they are. *Now apply these to yourself:*

- I will be kind to myself because I am having a bad day.
- I will look after myself because I am not very well.
- I will encourage my own development and growth.
- I will eat the right foods to remain healthy.
- I will ensure that I exercise so that I strengthen my body.
- I will remember that I am beautiful/handsome and that I am unique.
- I will raise my own self-esteem by reminding myself that I am important and have a bright future ahead.
- I will look after myself because I know that I need to today.

(*You can add more but this list is a guide to start from*).

Following on from this chapter are three case studies of fellow sufferers who have also, largely, recovered from ME and Fibro. Through their different experiences you will see the various ways ME and Fibro affect lives, but also how different people begin, approach and succeed in recovery.

Notes

Notes

Chapter 11

Recovery Stories

"Sometimes it takes a wake-up call, doesn't it, to alert us to the fact that we're hurrying through our lives instead of actually living them; that we're living the fast life instead of the good life. And I think, that for many people, that wake-up call takes the form of an illness."
Carl Honore, Canadian Journalist

Living with ME and Fibro can be extremely debilitating. There are people who never recover. There are those who stay ill for many, many years. A person I met recently said they had been ill for nearly thirty years. Can you imagine being ill for that length of time?

I have written this book to say that for the most part you CAN recover. On your road to recovery, life will never be the same. If, for example, you used to run a marathon, you may have to compromise slightly by, instead, doing a shorter run or even a walk. Let yourself build back up slowly. The people below, like myself, have also experienced recovery and are now living their lives to the full. Read their stories; they are inspirational!

Helen – Ask for Help

I am based in UK. I am thirty-three and have suffered from Fibro for ten years plus. Since I was young I've had illnesses that have led up to my being ill with Fibro. At seventeen, I was diagnosed with IBS. When I was at university, there was an epidemic of mumps. I had not had a booster for mumps and ended up catching it. It was later that the doctors also diagnosed me with post-viral fatigue.

A year later, Fibromyalgia started in my lower back and I was in extreme pain. I could not sit down for more than five minutes due to pain and swelling. I was sent home from work, my back was boiling hot and I had stabbing, pulsing pains. I drove to my parents' and then to the doctor's. I was given painkillers and anti-spasm tablets. I could not sleep. The next day the pain was going down my arms and neck. I went back to the doctor's and this time I was given anti-histamines, in case it was an allergic reaction. I was finding it difficult to breathe. So, I went to Selly Oak Hospital Accident & Emergency Department. After an ECG, nothing was found to be wrong with my heart. They realised the problem was muscular and was affecting the muscles in my heart, so they injected me with more anti-histamines. I had difficulty getting to sleep, only having about two hours total. I could not eat and could not even lift my head.

The tablets I was given made me ill as I was not digesting them properly, so I was just being sick. After some time, my GP suggested my illness might be Fibromyalgia. I was referred to a rheumatologist but had to wait for the appointment for several months, and by then was totally stiff. They did tests for everything: nerve damage, muscle diseases, blood tests and electro tests. I was not able to talk properly. I was put on Amitriptyline, which felt like an out-of-body experience, and I was told to go gluten-free.

The most challenging part of the illness was the depressive part.

On my road to recovery I found out about hydrotherapy, pain management and had physiotherapy too. Prior to being ill, I climbed Snowdon in August; by October I was unable to walk. My family were very supportive. I needed help to walk, even to get dressed, but gradually I learnt to adapt to life and regain control through a well-being coach. She especially helped me with accepting that I was ill and she taught me how to re-train my brain, to be more positive.

I am, now, much more active and I write a blog which supports hundreds of people with Chronic Fatigue and Fibro all over the world. I am proud of how far I have come.

It is people like Helen, who have suffered through similar experiences, that I love to help and provide my coaching services. Go to my website for more details.

Health tip for the mind: Do not be ashamed, or too proud, to ask for help and support.

Henry – Good Enough Will Do

I was diagnosed in 2008. I had been suffering complete exhaustion, brain fog and chest pain for over a year.

I had glandular fever when I was twenty and suffered post viral fatigue for about 10 years following this. Although this improved during my thirties, about every two years I suffered with some sort of non-specific illness, (albeit with similar symptoms) which required me to take to my bed for a couple of weeks.

I had a chest infection when I was fifty-three, which did not entirely clear up, and struggled with getting more and more exhausted for about six months (with an extremely stressful job and a sick elderly parent) before finally collapsing. I believe that, ultimately, my illness dates back to my glandular fever, even though I have not had it since the 1970s. Today, I am about 70% recovered, although I now have a completely different lifestyle.

Pacing and taking my level of activity down (and keeping it down) to far lower than I believed was necessary, was vital to my recovery. My occupational health doctor told me, in 2008, that I needed to find a level of activity I could manage every day. It took me a long time to do that and accept that it needed to remain low. Once I was able to sustain that, my energy levels started to grow.

I previously thrived on stress but have found myself unable to deal with either stress or negativity since. Therefore, I have removed stressful things, as much as possible, from my life.

CBT with a GOOD therapist, and I cannot stress the word 'good' sufficiently, was wonderful. My first experience was negative and detrimental to my recovery. Once I had found a good therapist, who I could relate to, and who had a good understanding of my illness, I started to improve. I still see him intermittently, if I feel I am heading towards a relapse, and he never fails to help me get back on track.

I now travel all over the world and enjoy the best of life. I also volunteer a lot and helping others and giving back to the community means a lot to me.

Health tip for your spirit: Remember, you do not have to be perfect at everything, good enough will do.

Christine – Stay True

I have been unwell for just over seven years. I developed a virus, suddenly. I remember that day clearly. I had typical flu-like symptoms, but without a high fever. I just could not recover from the virus. I kept trying to go back to work, but by early May I had to give in, and, initially, took four weeks off to rest and recuperate. Those four weeks turned into twelve months. I pushed myself to get back to work at that stage, or the alternative was that I would lose my job.

I now know one of the triggers for my illness was getting the swine flu jab, which I had in November 2009 (in order to keep me healthy, ironically!). I never felt well from the day I received that injection onwards, and it was all a bit of a puzzle to me.

As a member of the medical profession, the diagnosis slowly dawned on me and, in May, I thought I must have post-viral fatigue (PVFS). My GP was very supportive and investigated me thoroughly and agreed to refer me to a consultant physician, to see if any further light could be shed. All investigations, frustratingly, came back as normal, so I was left bewildered and felt extremely alone. The PVFS went on and became ME. I noticed no improvement, and was, in fact, getting worse.

I was very fortunate to find a local support group, run by two people who had fully recovered from ME. This gave me hope! I am a very determined person, and I felt that if they could recover then so could I. This led me along the natural healing route, with a focus on: dietary changes, meditation and holistic therapies. This opened up my eyes to a whole new world in relation to healing.

My Christian faith has been extremely important to me and a strong anchor in the midst of my storm. I am so grateful that I had deep roots in God before all this started.

I have been well enough to work part time for the last six years, though I have had to pace myself very carefully to achieve this. I do not consider myself quite fully recovered just yet, but those who see how I live my life would probably disagree!

These illnesses have forced me to stop and re-evaluate my life. Prior to getting ill, I was always busy, took on too much and did not consider the value of rest. However, I have learnt how to pace myself and really enjoy living life at a calmer pace. I am very grateful to my family and friends, who have been a constant support to me throughout my illness.

My work in the medical field continues to help and support many people. I go to the gym a lot, swimming is my favourite! My relationship with God has deepened too. I feel very blessed!

Health tip for the spirit: Be in tune with your creator, say a prayer of thanks every day.

There is no reason why you cannot achieve a similar kind of recovery to that of Helen, Henry, Christine and myself. There were times that we thought our lives were over and we could not picture ourselves ever feeling well again. However, by incorporating small, consistent changes into our lives we successfully unlocked the door to our recovery. In the next chapter, I will be summing up everything that I have discussed in this book and leave you with the tools and techniques to apply to your life that will get you feeling healthy and happy again.

Notes

Notes

Chapter 12

Step 9 – Leave Room for Margin Space

"Your health is your wealth,
so give yourself margin space each day."

Give Yourself Room

I hope from my story, and the stories in the previous chapters, that you can see that for a lot of people it has been possible to overcome and recover. You can have a wonderful, normal life again. Even if this life does not look exactly the same as before. It will be a life of good health, with great self-esteem, bursting with meaning, purpose, happiness and fulfilment.

Now, life, for those of us who have recovered, is not attempting to get as many things done in one day or trying to pack in as much as we can. You know, on a normal writing page, there is room at the top, bottom and to the sides, and these spaces are called margins? Well, I now give myself 'margin space.' You need to make space in your life for margins. Choose to live mindfully and stop to smell the roses.

When I need more rest one day, I have it. If I want to go out for a walk at mid-day, or in the morning, I give myself this flexibility. This means that I stay more energised and pain-free. When I need to take my mum to the hospital for an appointment, and cannot work for the rest of the day, or I need to attend a meeting at school for my children, and do not read my emails, I do so without guilt. This is because I give myself lots of 'margin space' within each day and within each week. Identify time when you are at your peak, and feel really well and give yourself margin space. **Do not**, and I repeat **do not,** deplete yourself of all your energy when you are feeling well.

Flexibility is the key to going forward. You have to be able to pace yourself. Listen to your body. That is when you live the dream. The dream of being well again.

Have a Positive Mental Attitude

Take ownership of how you feel and the actions you take. Fear tries to put false assumptions on us and convinces us that the outcomes of our actions will be negative. If you keep feeling down about your ill health, and do not focus on finding some positives, your attitude will likely stay negative. This results in feeling more ill for a longer period of time. You will have become your thoughts. However, a positive mental attitude is a huge asset and lends itself to you feeling well.

Imagine yourself healthy, wealthy and happy or whatever else you want to be. This vision will help you to achieve those targets, maybe not today or tomorrow but eventually. Especially if you set goals to help make this happen.

Get Support

You do not have to do this alone. Do not feel guilty about asking for help. Get friends and family to help you with your positive thinking. A well-being life coach, like myself, can help take the steps to recovery. This will be a huge boost for you and those who care about you.

To get through this illness, you will need both the support of others and, I believe, Divine help too. I ensure that I am in tune with the spiritual aspect of my life, always. We need to turn to our inner strength, a strength that comes from our spirit. If your spirit is full of hope, love and peace, it is easier to overcome the challenges you are facing.

Having Faith

The Good Book says: "Without faith, it is impossible..." Therefore, faith is important. You must BELIEVE. How does one put faith into a situation, when you are in despair and cannot see the way out? You must have hope, love and peace. Where do hope, love and peace come from? I believe they come from our creator, God Himself. Ask Him for these things and for help, guidance, direction and support.

It is important to believe that light will overcome the darkness, and you will get well again. Do not lose that hope. There may be days, when all hope has gone. I am here to tell you, that things can and will get better.

Notes

Get in Touch with Paulette Kumar

Working with people is what brings joy to my heart and purpose to my days. I love seeing happy, radiant and confident people. I love what I do. Having ME and Fibro has been difficult for me, and so many others, and has impacted on our lives enormously. However, I have greatly recovered and now I am excited to share what I learnt on my own journey of recovery with you, so that you too may overcome the difficult times.

After many years of coaching clients, I now specialise in providing help and support to those who are faced with low self-esteem and chronic illnesses. I hope this book has taught you to look at illnesses from a new perspective, a place of hope.

If you would like to access more of my resources and learn more about many of the things I have explored in this book, then visit my website: paulettekumar.com.

Search for Paulette Kumar online at www.paulettekumar.com. You can find me on Facebook, YouTube, Twitter and LinkedIn. Or call me directly on +44 775 46 44 202.

About the Author

Paulette Kumar is an award-winning author, philanthropist and ordained church elder. Paulette has an international presence and has served for over 30 years in her church community, giving advice and motivational talks.

Paulette is the daughter of immigrants and lived in one of most socially deprived areas near Birmingham throughout her childhood. She was brought up by a single mother, who instilled in her the desire to do her best. She obtained an Honours Degree in Computing and other professional qualifications. She has worked in a variety of places, including Goldman Sachs in the heart of the Wall Street area of New York. She later became a Project Manager. This was a career to which she dedicated herself to bring about positive changes, both in the public and private sector.

In November 2008, she caught a virus which left her totally exhausted, extremely debilitated and unable to work. Known to some as 'Yuppie Flu', she was diagnosed with Chronic Fatigue Syndrome / Myalgic Encephalomyelitis (M.E.) and Fibromyalgia.

She became housebound and was too weak to do the simplest of tasks and this lead to depression. Paulette found that the pharmaceutical drugs she was prescribed caused unpleasant side effects and she found this intolerable. Her strength of character helped her to address the situation in a positive way, by finding natural alternatives that would help her to recover from her illnesses.

She is now a Certified Life Breakthrough Coach™, who coaches and teaches people all over the world how they too can overcome debilitating illnesses. Her plethora of knowledge and advice regarding nutrition, stress-management, spirituality, sleep and holistic remedies will guide you to the happy and fulfilled life that you want.

In her book, she gives practical advice on ways that you can improve your health by sharing all of the knowledge she has spent over decades exploring and the changes she has implemented into her own life.

You can find her giving seminars and energy tips online on Facebook, through her website (www.paulettekumar.com), numerous programmes and over social media. Her motivational talks and coaching services empower thousands of people, from all walks of life.

Paulette lives in the curry capital of England, Birmingham, with her husband of over 20 years and her two children. She loves sun, sea and laughter, and writes down at least five things she is grateful for every day. Paulette loves to travel and is happy to make the journey to help you to enhance your life.

You can find Coach Paulette Kumar on Facebook, YouTube, Twitter and LinkedIn.

Paulette is available for delivering keynote presentations, motivational talks, seminars and tv and radio appearances to appropriate audiences. For rates and availability, please contact her directly on:
Telephone: +44 775 46 44 202
Email: coachpaulettekumar@gmail.com
Website: www.paulettekumar.com

To order more books please visit www.amazon.com

Finally, if you have been inspired by this book then buy a copy for someone you care for or pass this one along to them. It will make a huge difference to their life!

Because everyone deserves good health!

Notes

38784230R00065

Printed in Poland
by Amazon Fulfillment
Poland Sp. z o.o., Wrocław